Michael Waltz

Michael George Glen Waltz was born on January 31, 1974, in Boynton Beach, Florida, and grew up in Jacksonville. From a young age, he showed signs of leadership and a strong commitment to service, traits that would define his career in the years to come. After completing high school, Waltz pursued higher education at the Virginia Military Institute, where he earned a Bachelor of Arts degree in international studies. His time at VMI prepared him for the military career that lay ahead, and upon graduation, he was commissioned as a second lieutenant in the U.S. Army.

Waltz's military career would become a significant part of his life, shaping not only his worldview but also his future in politics. After commissioning, he graduated from the rigorous U.S. Army Ranger School and was selected to join the ranks of the elite Green Berets. Over the next 26 years, Waltz served as a Special Forces officer, deploying on multiple tours to Afghanistan, the Middle East, and Africa. His courage and leadership in combat earned him numerous accolades, including four Bronze Stars, two of which were awarded for valor.

In addition to his time on the front lines, Waltz also held key policy roles in the U.S. government. He worked in the Pentagon as a defense policy director under Secretaries of Defense Donald Rumsfeld and Robert Gates, and later served as the vice president's counterterrorism advisor in the White House. His experiences in both combat and policy led him to write a book titled Warrior Diplomat: A Green Beret's Battles from Washington to Afghanistan, chronicling his unique journey as both a soldier and a diplomat.

Waltz's drive to continue serving his country led him to enter the political arena. In 2018, he ran for Florida's 6th congressional district, which covers the eastern coast of Florida from the southern suburbs of Jacksonville to New Smyrna Beach, including Daytona Beach. The district was left open when Ron DeSantis, the incumbent, ran for and won the governorship of Florida. Waltz secured the Republican nomination and went on to defeat Democratic candidate Nancy Soderberg, a former deputy national security advisor and United Nations representative. With 56.3% of the vote, Waltz won his seat in Congress and has since been re-elected multiple times.

As a U.S. representative, Waltz has continued to focus on issues related to national security, foreign policy, and military affairs. He became the first Green Beret ever elected to Congress, bringing with him a unique perspective on both global conflicts and domestic security. His strong stance on the War in Afghanistan and his belief in the need for a long-term strategy to combat extremism earned him respect among his colleagues. Waltz also emerged as one of Congress's most vocal critics of China, warning about the growing threat posed by the Chinese Communist Party and advocating for policies to counter Chinese influence, including calling for a boycott of the 2022 Winter Olympics in Beijing over human rights abuses.

Waltz has served on several key committees, including the House Armed Services Committee and the House Foreign Affairs Committee. He played an instrumental role in passing legislation aimed at reducing U.S. reliance on foreign critical minerals and ensuring the transparency of foreign funding in American universities, particularly in response to Chinese espionage concerns.

Outside of Congress, Waltz's business acumen came to the forefront when he co-founded Metis Solutions, an analytics and training company specializing in strategic analysis and intelligence support. Metis Solutions grew into a successful enterprise with operations in several global locations, including Afghanistan. In 2020, the company was sold for $92 million.

On the personal side, Waltz is married to Julia Nesheiwat, a combat veteran and former homeland security advisor under the Trump administration. Together, they have two children, and they reside in St. Johns County, Florida. Waltz also has a teenage daughter from a previous relationship.

Waltz's political journey continues as he navigates the complexities of the modern geopolitical landscape while remaining dedicated to the values he learned as a soldier. Through his military service, business ventures, and political leadership, Michael Waltz has remained a steadfast advocate for the defense and security of the United States.

Early Life and Education

Michael George Glen Waltz was born on January 31, 1974, in Boynton Beach, Florida, but spent much of his formative years in Jacksonville. Growing up in a military family, he was instilled with a sense of duty and patriotism from an early age. This sense of responsibility led him to pursue higher education at the Virginia Military Institute, where he earned a Bachelor of Arts degree in international studies. Upon graduation, he was commissioned as a second lieutenant in the United States Army, embarking on a journey that would define much of his life.

Military Career

Waltz's military career has been distinguished and impactful. After his commission, he graduated from Ranger School and was selected to become a Green Beret, serving as a Special Forces officer across the globe. Over the course of his 26-plus years in the Army, he completed multiple tours in Afghanistan, the Middle East, and Africa, where he demonstrated exceptional leadership and bravery in combat. His valor earned him four Bronze Stars, including two for valor, marking him as a combat-decorated officer.

In addition to his combat service, Waltz played a significant role in shaping defense policy at the highest levels. He worked at the Pentagon as a defense policy director under Secretaries of Defense Donald Rumsfeld and Robert Gates. Later, he served as the Vice President's counterterrorism advisor at the White House, providing strategic insight and guidance on critical national security matters.

In 2010, Waltz co-founded Metis Solutions, a defense contracting firm that provided strategic analysis and training. His entrepreneurial efforts culminated in the sale of the company for $92 million in November 2020, marking a successful transition from military service to the private sector.

Political Career

In 2018, Waltz ventured into politics, running for Florida's 6th congressional district, a seat previously held by Ron DeSantis. With a campaign focused on national security and military readiness, he emerged victorious in the Republican primary against John Ward and Fred Costello, securing his position in Congress by defeating Democratic nominee Nancy Soderberg with 56.31% of the vote in the general election.

Since taking office on January 3, 2019, Waltz has established himself as a prominent voice in Congress, particularly on issues related to national security and foreign policy. As the first Green Beret elected to Congress, he brings a unique perspective to legislative discussions. His service on various committees, including the House Armed Services Committee and the Permanent Select Committee on Intelligence, positions him at the forefront of critical national discussions.

Waltz is known for his hawkish stance on China, asserting that the U.S. is in a Cold War with the Chinese Communist Party. He was the first member of Congress to call for a full boycott of the 2022 Winter Olympics in Beijing, citing human rights abuses against the Uyghur population. He actively promotes legislation aimed at reducing U.S. reliance on foreign minerals and securing American universities from espionage threats.

Personal Life

Michael Waltz is married to Julia Nesheiwat, a combat veteran who served in various capacities across three presidential administrations. Together, they have a blended family, including Waltz's teenage daughter and a child they share. The couple resides in St. Johns County, Florida, where they continue to be active in their community.

Waltz is also an accomplished author. His book, Warrior Diplomat: A Green Beret's Battles from Washington to Afghanistan, shares insights from his unique experiences in the military and government, highlighting the intersection of diplomacy and defense.

As a congressman, military officer, and family man, Michael Waltz embodies a commitment to service that spans both his personal and professional life, making a lasting impact on his constituents and the nation.

Legislative Initiatives and Accomplishments

Throughout his tenure in Congress, Michael Waltz has championed various legislative initiatives aimed at enhancing national security, improving veterans' services, and supporting the military community. Some of his notable legislative achievements include:

National Security Legislation: Waltz has introduced and supported measures to strengthen the U.S. military's capabilities and readiness. He advocates for increased funding for defense programs and has pushed for modernization of military equipment to ensure that American forces remain prepared for contemporary threats.

Veterans' Affairs: As a vocal advocate for veterans, Waltz has worked on legislation aimed at improving access to healthcare and benefits for former service members. He has focused on issues such as mental health support, suicide prevention, and ensuring that veterans receive the resources they need to transition successfully into civilian life.

Counterterrorism Efforts: Waltz has been a strong proponent of robust counterterrorism measures, emphasizing the need for a comprehensive strategy to combat both domestic and international terrorism. He has supported increased funding for intelligence operations and the use of advanced technology to enhance national security.

Economic Development: Recognizing the importance of a strong economy to national security, Waltz has advocated for policies that promote job creation and economic growth. He has focused on supporting small businesses, advancing workforce development initiatives, and ensuring that American workers are equipped with the skills needed for the jobs of the future.

Foreign Policy Engagement: Waltz's background as a Green Beret informs his approach to foreign policy. He has emphasized the importance of diplomatic efforts alongside military readiness and has called for a strategic focus on threats posed by adversarial nations, particularly China and Russia. His engagement in foreign policy discussions reflects his commitment to protecting American interests abroad.

Community Involvement and Advocacy

Outside of his congressional duties, Waltz remains actively engaged in his community and various philanthropic initiatives. He frequently participates in events supporting veterans, active-duty military personnel, and their families. Waltz also collaborates with local organizations to promote educational programs aimed at fostering leadership skills among youth, emphasizing the importance of civic engagement and service.

Waltz's commitment to public service extends beyond politics; he often shares his experiences and insights through public speaking engagements, educational forums, and media appearances. His unique perspective as a combat veteran and policymaker resonates with audiences, allowing him to inspire future generations of leaders.

Awards and Recognitions

Michael Waltz's service and contributions have not gone unnoticed. He has received numerous accolades and awards throughout his military and political careers, including:

Bronze Stars: Awarded for acts of heroism and meritorious service in a combat zone.

Department of Defense Distinguished Public Service Award: Recognizing exceptional service to the Department of Defense.

Various commendations from military organizations and veterans' groups for his advocacy and commitment to improving the lives of service members and their families.

Personal Interests and Hobbies

In his free time, Waltz enjoys outdoor activities, including hiking, fishing, and spending time with his family. He is an avid reader, often exploring topics related to military history, leadership, and foreign policy. He also enjoys engaging with his constituents through town hall meetings and social media, fostering a sense of connection and accountability.

Conclusion

Michael George Glen Waltz exemplifies a life dedicated to service, leadership, and advocacy. From his distinguished military career to his impactful role in Congress, he continues to champion the interests of his constituents and the nation. With a commitment to national security, veterans' affairs, and economic development, Waltz remains a prominent figure in American politics, inspiring others to follow in his footsteps of service and dedication. His journey reflects the values of integrity, courage, and commitment to the greater good, making him a respected leader both within and outside of the political arena.

Future Aspirations and Goals

As Michael Waltz looks ahead, he remains focused on addressing the pressing challenges facing his constituents and the nation. His aspirations include:

Strengthening National Defense: Waltz is committed to advocating for policies that enhance the capabilities of the U.S. military. He aims to push for increased investment in cutting-edge technologies, cyber defense, and intelligence operations to address emerging threats in a rapidly evolving global landscape.

Promoting Bipartisanship: Recognizing the importance of collaboration across party lines, Waltz seeks to foster a spirit of bipartisanship in Congress. He believes that addressing complex issues such as healthcare, immigration, and infrastructure requires cooperation and compromise from both sides of the aisle.

Advancing Veteran Services: Waltz's commitment to improving the lives of veterans remains a top priority. He plans to continue working on legislation that enhances access to healthcare, mental health services, and job training for veterans, ensuring that they receive the support they deserve after their service.

Economic Resilience: As the economy continues to face challenges, Waltz aims to promote policies that support small businesses and workforce development initiatives. He is particularly focused on enhancing opportunities for young people entering the job market, emphasizing the need for education and skills training that align with industry demands.

Community Engagement: Waltz understands the importance of staying connected with his constituents. He plans to continue hosting town hall meetings and community forums to listen to the concerns and ideas of the people he represents. By fostering open communication, he hopes to ensure that his legislative priorities align with the needs of the community.

Legacy of Leadership
Michael Waltz's journey from a Green Beret to a U.S. Congressman is a testament to his unwavering dedication to public service and leadership. His experiences have shaped his worldview and informed his approach to governance, making him a unique voice in Congress. As he continues to serve, he aspires to leave a lasting legacy of courage, resilience, and commitment to the American ideals of freedom and democracy.

Personal Life

Waltz resides in St. Augustine, Florida, with his wife, a dedicated educator, and their two children. He is an active member of his local community, often participating in events that support education, youth development, and veteran services. Waltz instills the values of service and leadership in his children, encouraging them to be engaged citizens and to appreciate the importance of giving back to their community.

In addition to his political and community endeavors, Waltz is passionate about fitness and outdoor activities. He enjoys spending quality time with his family, whether it's exploring Florida's natural beauty through hiking and camping or participating in community sports events.

Final Thoughts

Michael Waltz's journey reflects the belief that a life dedicated to service can create meaningful change in the world. As he navigates the complexities of political life, he remains committed to his core values of integrity, resilience, and compassion. Through his leadership, he aims to inspire others to engage in public service and contribute to the betterment of society.

Waltz's story is one of determination and purpose, serving as a reminder that the actions of individuals—whether in the military, in politics, or in the community—can profoundly impact the lives of others. With a clear vision for the future, he continues to be a force for positive change, championing the causes he believes in and advocating for a brighter tomorrow for all Americans.

Commitment to Education and Innovation

Michael Waltz recognizes the vital role education plays in shaping the future of America. He believes that a strong educational system is essential for nurturing the next generation of leaders and innovators. To this end, he is dedicated to promoting policies that enhance educational opportunities for all students. His focus areas include:

STEM Education: Waltz advocates for increased investment in Science, Technology, Engineering, and Mathematics (STEM) education. He believes that equipping students with these skills is essential for preparing them for the jobs of the future, especially in a technology-driven economy.

School Choice: As a proponent of school choice, Waltz supports initiatives that give parents the freedom to choose the best educational options for their children. He believes that empowering families with choices can lead to better educational outcomes and promote competition among schools.

Vocational Training: Waltz emphasizes the importance of vocational training and apprenticeships as viable pathways for students who may not pursue traditional college degrees. He believes that by promoting these options, we can meet the demands of various industries and ensure a skilled workforce.

Supporting Teachers: Recognizing the crucial role that educators play, Waltz is committed to advocating for policies that support teachers, including competitive salaries, professional development opportunities, and resources needed to succeed in the classroom.

Advocacy for Healthcare Improvements

Waltz believes that access to quality healthcare is a fundamental right and aims to address the challenges facing the healthcare system. His efforts include:

Mental Health Services: Acknowledging the growing mental health crisis, particularly among veterans and young people, Waltz champions increased funding for mental health services and initiatives aimed at reducing stigma surrounding mental health issues.

Affordable Care: He is committed to exploring solutions that make healthcare more affordable for families, including promoting competition among providers and addressing prescription drug pricing.

Veterans' Healthcare: Given his background and commitment to veteran services, Waltz is a vocal advocate for improving the Veterans Affairs (VA) healthcare system. He seeks to enhance access to quality care and reduce bureaucratic hurdles for veterans seeking assistance.

Engagement in Local and National Issues

Waltz understands that effective leadership requires an awareness of both local and national issues. He prioritizes engagement with his constituents to ensure their voices are heard in Congress. His approach includes:

Regular Town Halls: Waltz hosts regular town hall meetings to discuss pressing issues, gather feedback, and answer questions from constituents. This commitment to transparency fosters a sense of community involvement and encourages civic engagement.

Collaboration with Local Leaders: He actively collaborates with local officials, business leaders, and community organizations to address specific needs within his district. By working together, they can develop innovative solutions to improve the quality of life for residents.

National Advocacy: Waltz is also engaged in national issues that affect his district, such as environmental concerns, disaster preparedness, and economic development. He works to secure federal resources and support for local initiatives that align with national priorities.

Legacy of Compassion and Resilience

As Michael Waltz continues his journey in public service, his legacy is one of compassion, resilience, and commitment to the principles of democracy. He exemplifies the belief that true leadership is rooted in empathy and understanding. Waltz strives to be a representative who listens to his constituents and takes their concerns to heart, ensuring that their voices resonate in the halls of power.

His journey from a decorated Green Beret to a U.S. Congressman is a powerful testament to the impact one individual can make in the lives of many. Waltz's dedication to service, both in the military and in Congress, serves as an inspiration to others, demonstrating that the values of honor, integrity, and commitment can drive positive change in society.

Conclusion

In conclusion, Michael Waltz's biography is marked by a deep-seated commitment to public service, leadership, and advocacy for the American people. His journey reflects the ideals of courage, perseverance, and dedication to the greater good. As he continues to navigate the complexities of political life, he remains steadfast in his mission to serve his constituents and advocate for policies that promote a brighter future for all Americans. Through his unwavering commitment, he hopes to inspire others to engage in public service and contribute to the ongoing narrative of democracy and civic responsibility.

Environmental Stewardship and Climate Resilience

In addition to his focus on national security, education, and healthcare, Michael Waltz has shown a commitment to environmental issues, especially those impacting Florida. Representing a state that is vulnerable to climate change, rising sea levels, and extreme weather events, Waltz understands the need for proactive measures to safeguard both the environment and the economy. His approach to environmental policy includes:

Preserving Florida's Ecosystems: Waltz has advocated for federal investment to protect Florida's unique ecosystems, including the Everglades, which serve as vital natural resources and support the state's tourism industry. He supports initiatives aimed at restoring wetlands, improving water quality, and ensuring sustainable land use.

Water Management and Conservation: Water management is critical for Florida, particularly in the face of frequent hurricanes and flooding. Waltz has supported measures to improve water infrastructure, reduce pollution in waterways, and address issues like toxic algae blooms, which have harmed local economies and ecosystems.

Climate Resilience: Recognizing the threat posed by rising sea levels and increasingly severe storms, Waltz advocates for climate resilience initiatives. This includes supporting coastal defense projects, such as improving seawalls and flood barriers, to protect communities from the impact of extreme weather events.

Renewable Energy: Although Waltz maintains a pragmatic stance on energy, acknowledging the ongoing role of traditional energy sources, he also supports expanding renewable energy technologies. He encourages investment in solar and wind energy, as well as research into sustainable alternatives that can reduce America's reliance on fossil fuels while promoting economic growth.

Championing National Security and Defense

Michael Waltz's extensive military background shapes much of his policy stance on defense and national security. As a combat veteran, his views are informed by firsthand experience in conflict zones, giving him a unique perspective on the global threats facing the U.S. He has become a strong advocate for:

Strengthening the Military: Waltz is a staunch supporter of maintaining a strong, well-funded military. He believes that continued investment in defense is necessary to ensure that the U.S. remains prepared to counter emerging threats from adversaries such as China, Russia, and rogue states.

Supporting Service Members and Veterans: Waltz advocates for policies that enhance the welfare of military personnel and veterans, particularly in the areas of mental health, family support, and career transition. He supports reforms aimed at improving the VA healthcare system and providing resources to help veterans integrate into civilian life.

Counterterrorism and National Security Strategy: Drawing on his experience as a Green Beret and counterterrorism advisor, Waltz is focused on strengthening America's counterterrorism efforts both domestically and abroad. He supports measures to combat the spread of extremism and terrorism, including enhanced intelligence-sharing, cybersecurity initiatives, and diplomatic engagement with global partners.

Modernizing the Military: Waltz also supports modernizing the U.S. military to address new forms of warfare, such as cyberattacks and information warfare. He believes that the military must be equipped with cutting-edge technology and strategies to confront the increasingly sophisticated tactics used by America's adversaries.

Leadership in Foreign Affairs

In addition to his national security work, Waltz has taken a keen interest in foreign policy. His experience working in counterterrorism under both Republican and Democratic administrations provides him with a bipartisan outlook on international affairs. Waltz's foreign policy priorities include:

Maintaining Alliances: Waltz is a strong advocate for maintaining America's global alliances, including NATO. He believes that these partnerships are essential for preserving global stability and protecting U.S. interests abroad. He supports efforts to strengthen ties with traditional allies while encouraging burden-sharing among partner nations.

Confronting China's Influence: Waltz has been a vocal critic of China's growing influence on the global stage, particularly in terms of economic competition, technological dominance, and military expansion. He supports policies aimed at countering Chinese aggression, especially in the Indo-Pacific region, and reducing America's economic reliance on Chinese goods.

Supporting Democracy and Human Rights: Waltz believes that the U.S. should be a leading voice in promoting democracy and human rights worldwide. He has supported efforts to hold authoritarian regimes accountable for human rights abuses, and he is a strong advocate for supporting democratic movements, especially in regions where freedom and individual rights are under threat.

Combatting Global Terrorism: Given his background in counterterrorism, Waltz is focused on ongoing efforts to dismantle terrorist networks and prevent the resurgence of groups like ISIS and al-Qaeda. He supports maintaining a presence in regions vulnerable to extremism and strengthening partnerships with foreign governments to address the root causes of terrorism.

The Path Forward: Inspiring Future Generations
Michael Waltz's career exemplifies his belief in public service as a vehicle for positive change. Whether through his military service, his work in Congress, or his community engagement, Waltz has consistently demonstrated a commitment to his principles and the people he serves.

Engaging with Young Leaders: Waltz is passionate about inspiring future generations to engage in public service and leadership. He frequently speaks at schools, universities, and civic organizations, encouraging young people to take an active role in shaping the future of their communities and their country.

Veteran Mentorship: As a veteran, Waltz understands the unique challenges faced by those transitioning from military to civilian life. He has been involved in mentorship programs for veterans, helping them navigate career opportunities and encouraging them to pursue leadership roles in business, government, and nonprofit sectors.

Service Above Self: Throughout his career, Waltz has embodied the ideal of "service above self." Whether on the battlefield or in the halls of Congress, he has consistently placed the needs of others ahead of his own, driven by a desire to protect and uplift his fellow citizens.

Conclusion

Michael George Glen Waltz's life is a testament to the power of leadership, service, and commitment to country. From his early days as a young man driven to serve in the Special Forces, to his role in Congress advocating for veterans, national security, education, and environmental protection, Waltz has demonstrated that public service is both a duty and a privilege.

As he continues to represent Florida in Congress, Waltz remains dedicated to the ideals that have guided him throughout his career: protecting American values, advancing policies that promote economic and social prosperity, and ensuring that future generations inherit a world that is secure, prosperous, and just.

In his ongoing work, Waltz exemplifies the kind of leadership that inspires confidence, and his legacy will undoubtedly be one of dedication, resilience, and unwavering patriotism.

Made in the USA
Monee, IL
04 January 2025